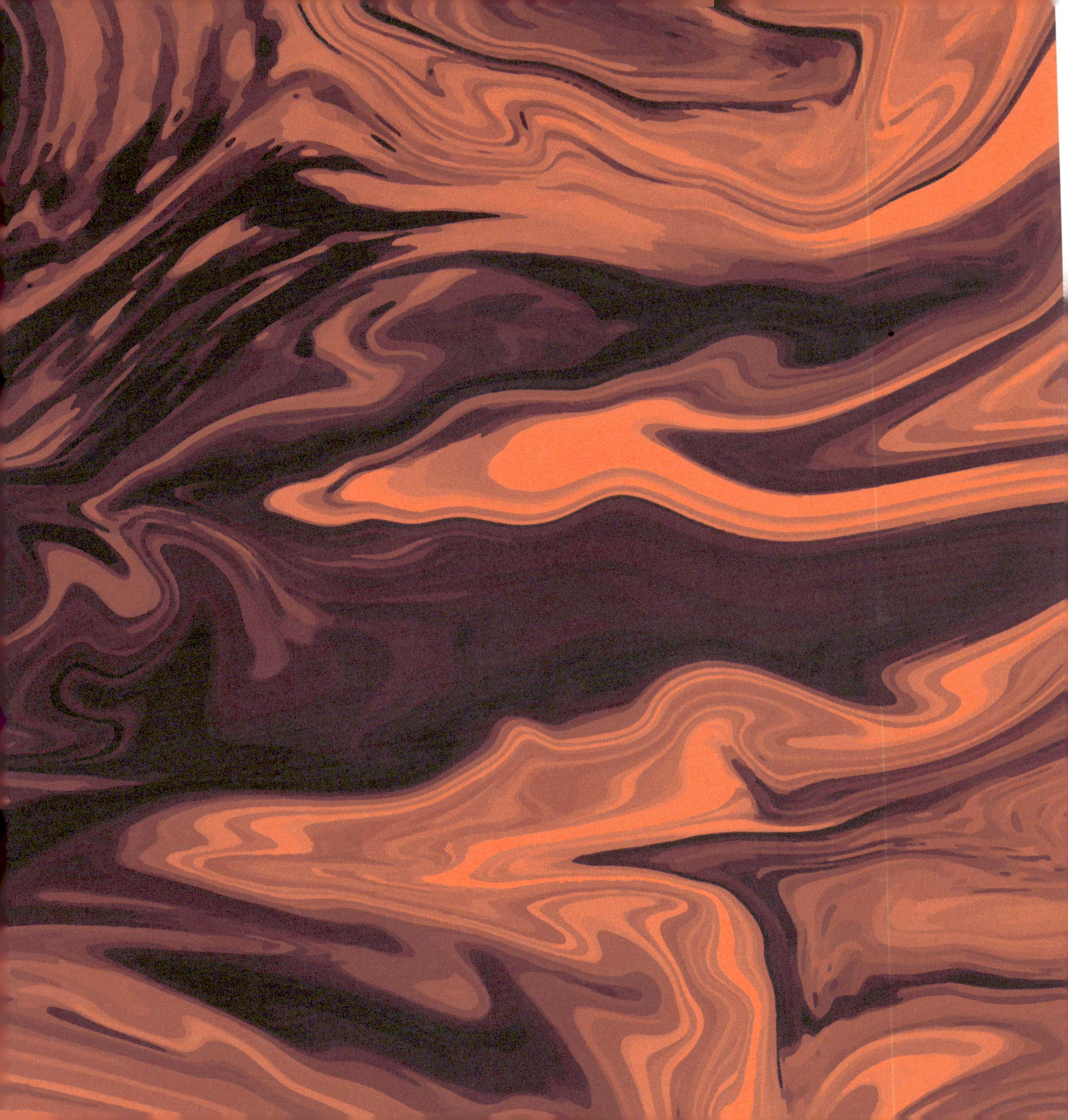

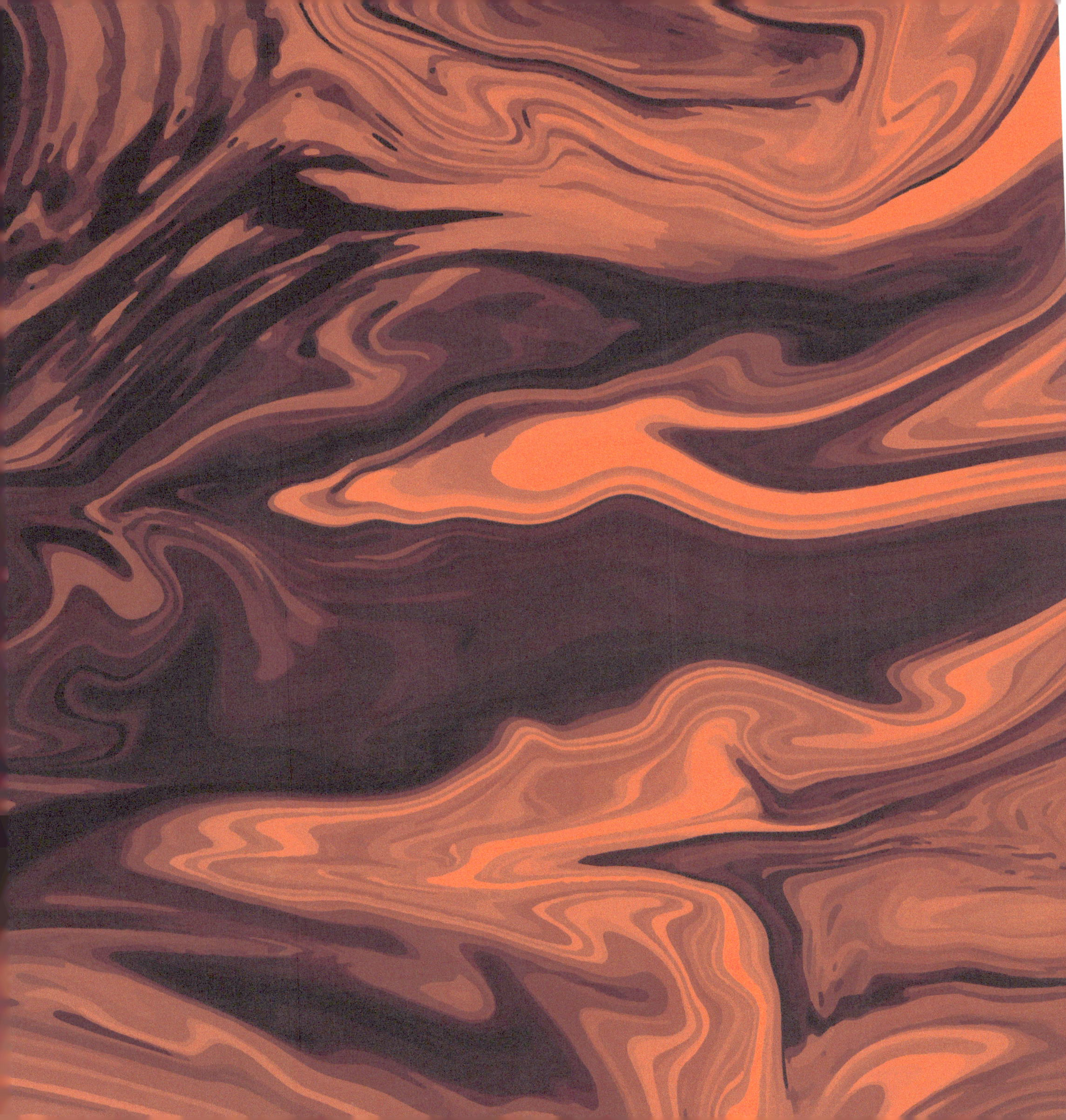

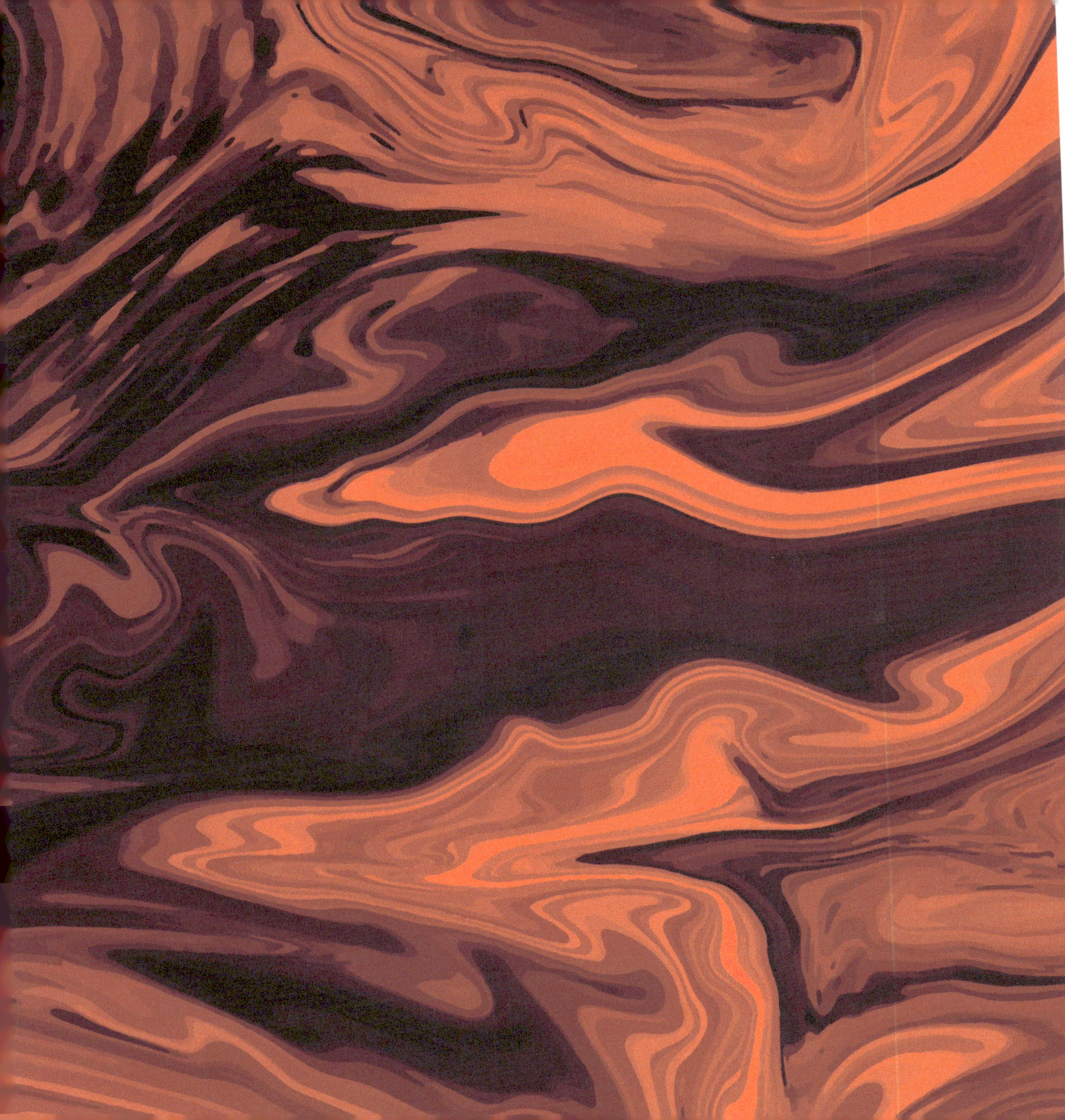

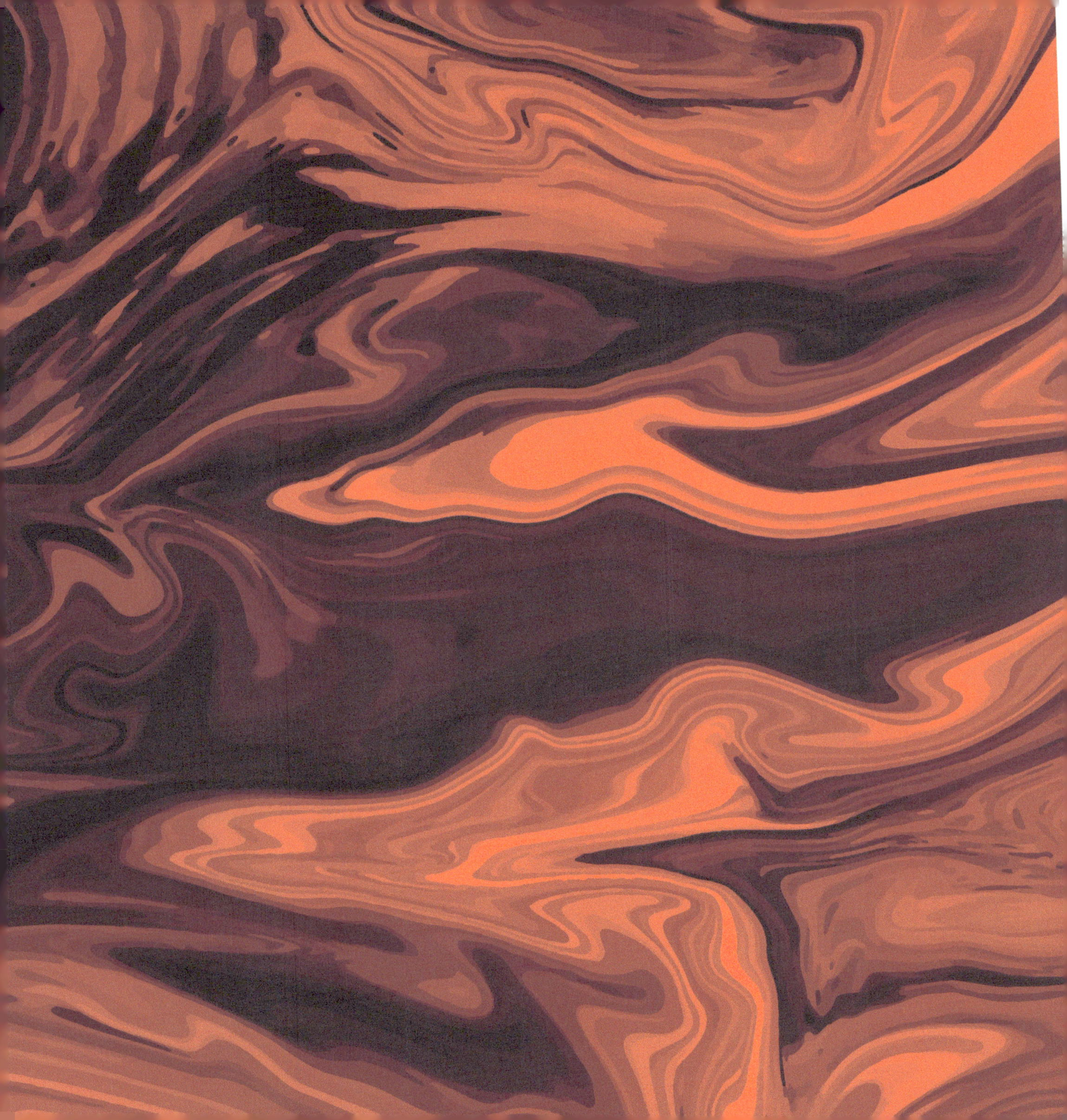

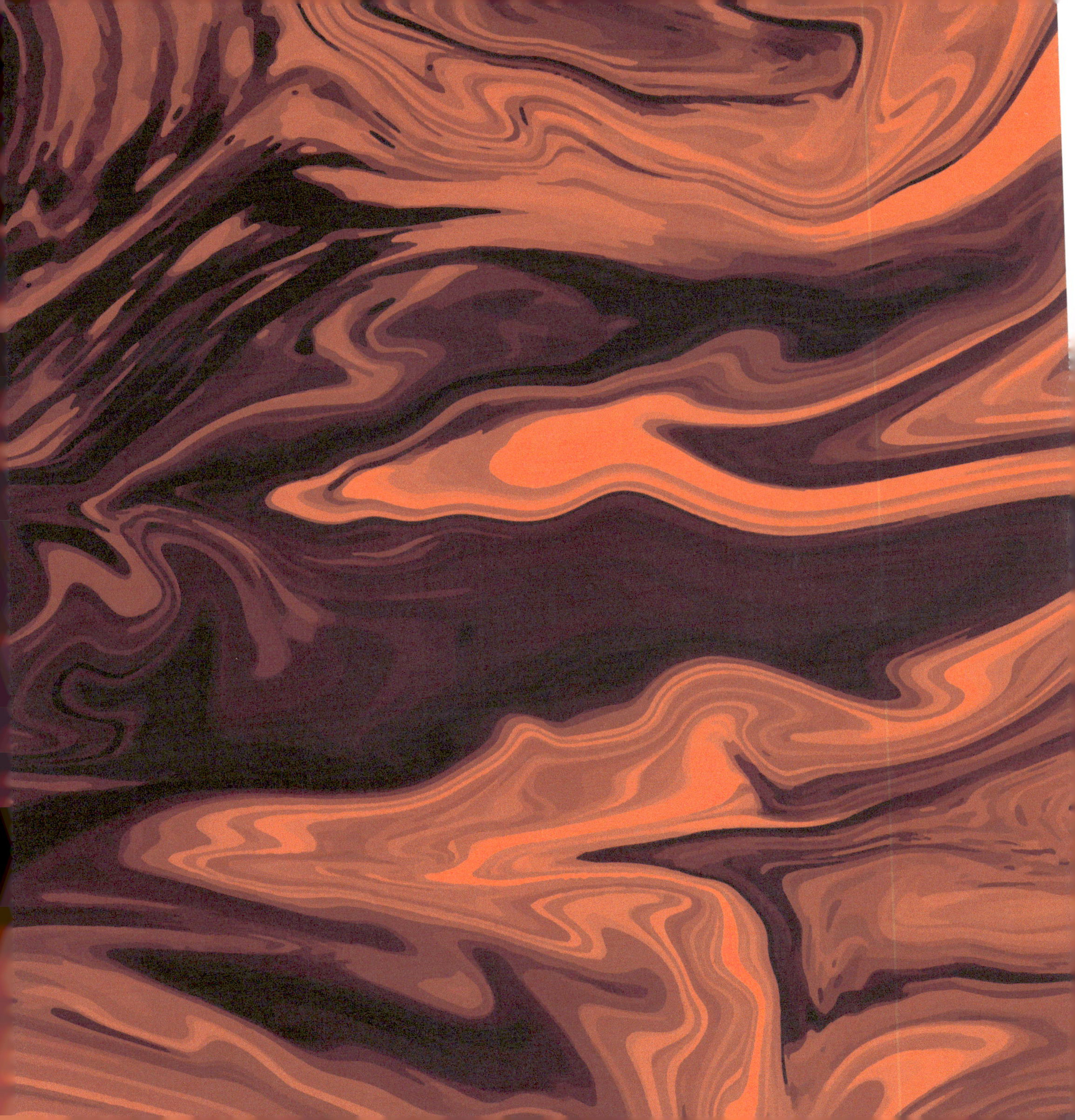

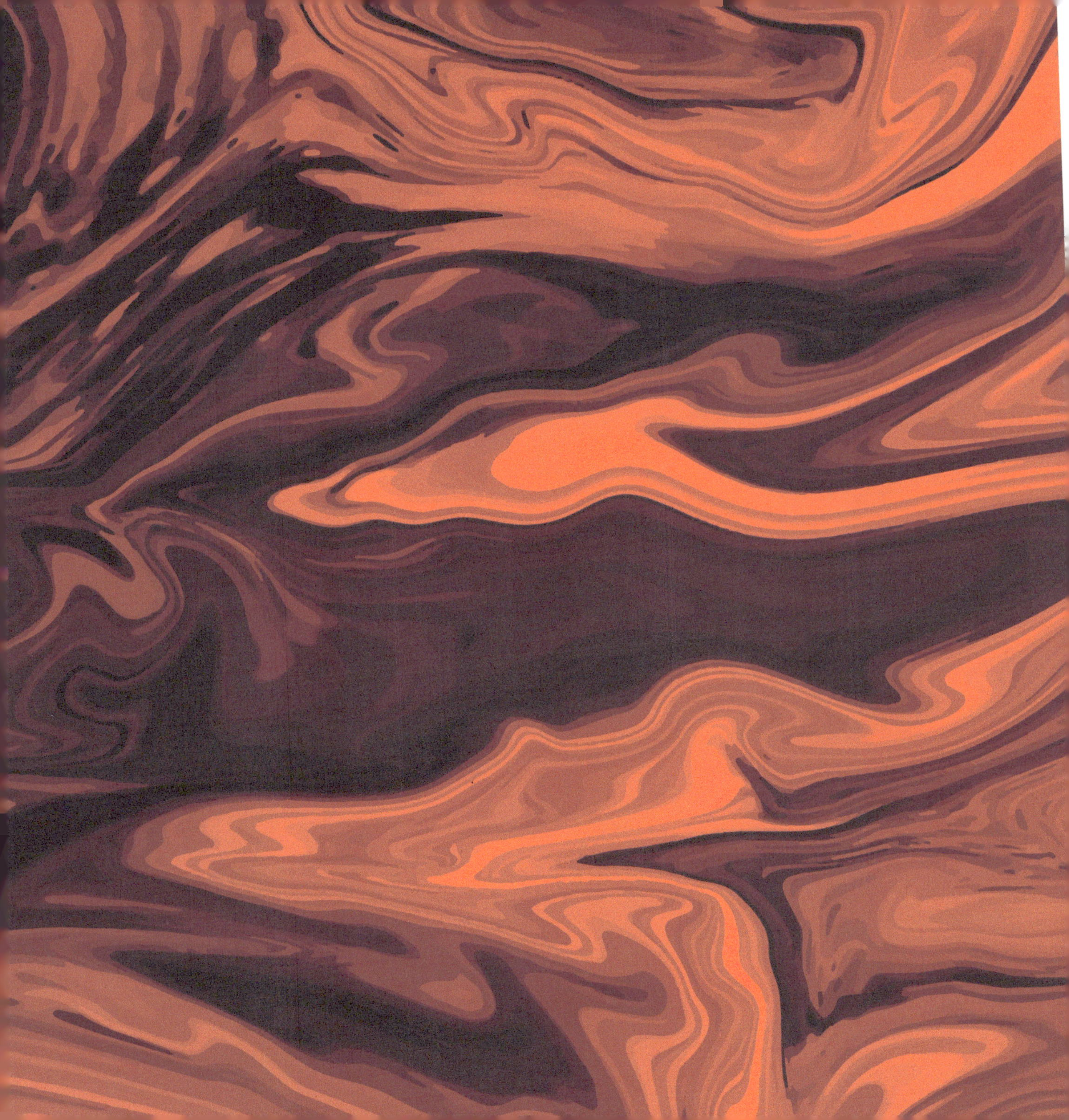

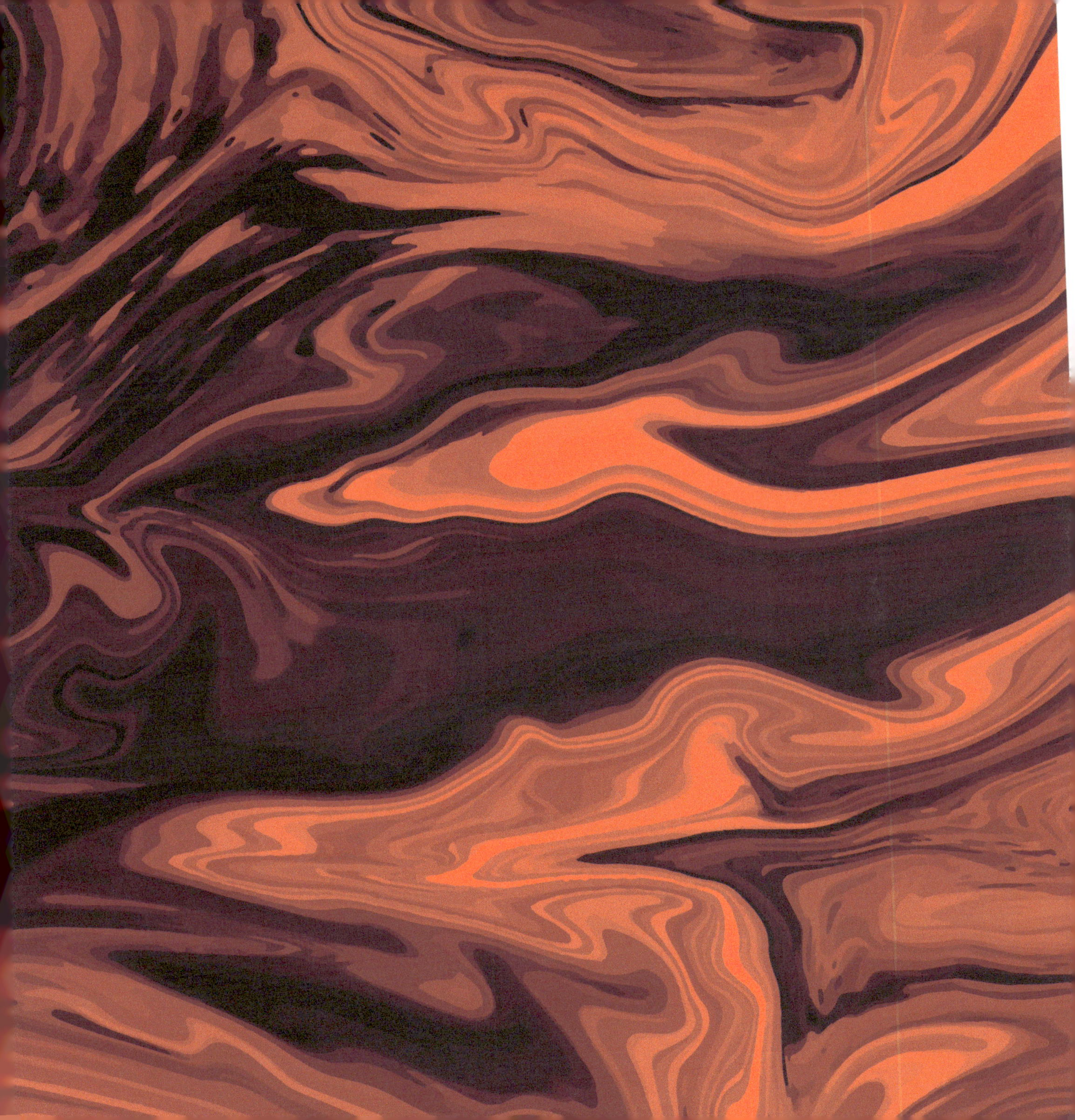

CPSIA information can be obtained
at www.ICGtesting.com
Printed in the USA
BVHW020943090221
599700BV00016B/138

9781953987280